Begin

Begin

First Steps
for the Journey of Faith

BOB FRANQUIZ

BakerBooks

a division of Baker Publishing Group
Grand Rapids, Michigan

© 2013 by Bob Franquiz

Published by Baker Books
a division of Baker Publishing Group
P.O. Box 6287, Grand Rapids, MI 49516-6287
www.bakerbooks.com

Printed in the United States of America

Library of Congress Cataloging-in-Publication Data is on file at the Library of Congress, Washington, DC.

ISBN 978-0-8010-1561-8

Unless otherwise indicated, Scripture quotations are from the *Holy Bible*, New Living Translation, copyright © 1996, 2004, 2007 by Tyndale House Foundation. Used by permission of Tyndale House Publishers, Inc., Carol Stream, Illinois 60188. All rights reserved.

Scripture quotations labeled Message are from *The Message* by Eugene H. Peterson, copyright © 1993, 1994, 1995, 2000, 2001, 2002. Used by permission of NavPress Publishing Group. All rights reserved.

Scripture quotations labeled NIV are from the Holy Bible, New International Version®. NIV®. Copyright © 1973, 1978, 1984, 2011 by Biblica, Inc.™ Used by permission of Zondervan. All rights reserved worldwide. www.zondervan.com

Scripture quotations labeled NKJV are from the New King James Version. Copyright © 1982 by Thomas Nelson, Inc. Used by permission. All rights reserved.

13   14   15   16   17   18   19   7   6   5   4   3   2   1

Contents

Introduction

My Story

*M*y spiritual journey began when I was young. My parents weren't very religious people, but they thought highly of religious education. From third through eighth grade, I attended a parochial school near my house. That's where I learned about God and different aspects of the Bible. I was taught various prayers to say at specific times, and I was educated on who the major players are in the Bible. I even participated in services that probably once had rich meaning but by the time I learned them had become routine and shallow.

I was taught *about* God, but I was never introduced *to* God. God was explained to me the way a teacher gives information about a former world leader or historic figure. I was taught that God is "out there somewhere" but was never told that he is close to me.

My parents are divorced. Each has been married more than once, which makes my family tree look like a two-year-old drew it. I have two sisters and a brother, but my two sisters aren't related. This felt odd to me as I was growing up—odd enough to make God seem distant to what mattered in my life. So I went through adolescence with a pseudo-faith. I believed in God. I even believed that Jesus was God's Son who died on a cross so I could be forgiven, but that never meant anything to me. "Faith" never crossed paths with real life—never, that is, until May 29, 1993.

A New Understanding

I was nineteen and visiting my older brother, who lives in Boston; he had given his life to Christ. Now, this confused me because I thought we were already Christian. I mean, we were Catholic, but I thought that it was all the same thing, the way Coke, Pepsi, and RC are all types of cola, just different flavors.

When I saw my brother and spent some time with him, I realized that our understandings of God were different. It's not that we believed differently; I was amazed at how much we agreed about spiritual things. When my brother spoke about God, he spoke as if he were talking about someone he knew, as if he and God had just gotten off the phone.

My understanding of God was based on facts. I knew about how he created the world in six days, how he once caused it to flood, and how he parted the Red Sea (okay, I got that from the movie *Bruce Almighty*, but it's in the Bible too). My brother talked about a new creation, a re-creation of a human life that yields itself to God. He spoke of a flood of forgiveness God sent in his direction because of what Jesus had done for him. He explained the miracles God performed in his life. For some reason, these things were more spectacular to me than a sea parting down the middle, maybe because they were more tangible.

I awoke the next morning in my brother's house, full of questions. I sat at his kitchen table, and we talked for the next few hours. He didn't just share facts about how Jesus died on the cross, how humans are sinners, and that the Bible is God's book. He told me how all these things matter today. He explained that, as a person, when I do something wrong, I become separated from God because I have failed to meet God's standard. But in his love, God sent Jesus to be the sacrifice that covered all sins I committed. Because of this act of love, through my faith in Jesus, I can spend eternity with God. Meanwhile, I can have a real life here on Earth, in a relationship with God. Through the sacrifice of Jesus, I am no longer separated from God.

I was confused. I told him, "But I already believe in God." Then he explained to me that there's a difference between faith and belief. We believe many things without putting our faith in them. How many smokers believe smoking is unhealthy? Most of them. But that belief doesn't change their habits. How many people believe that being over-weight isn't good for them? Most of them. Believing something is true and having the courage to take a step to walk in that truth are different things. That's where faith comes in.

Faith requires acting on the beliefs we have. This is where my brother and I were different. He had faith, and I had only a belief. So he invited me to pray and put my faith in Jesus and become a Christian. This wasn't an invitation into a religious system; I already had that. This was an invitation into a relationship, a connection with God. That's why God asks us to call him Father. It's a word of connection and relationship.

I decided to pray and ask Jesus to forgive me. I asked God to set my life on a new path and to give me peace. What's amazing is that he did! God changed my life. And if you're reading this, either God has done this in your life, or you want him to do it.

Welcome to Miami

A few days after becoming a Christian, I had to go home to Miami, where I lived with my mom and younger sister. I was nineteen and in college, but I didn't know any Christians or what to do with my newfound faith. I started attending a great church, and with the help of people there, I learned some basics of the Christian faith and steps to growing spiritually.

As I look back on my spiritual journey, I see five decisions that helped me tremendously in growing in my relationship with God. If you incorporate these into your life, they will help you immensely in your pursuit of knowing God and growing in your faith.

I Decided to Communicate with God Daily

We communicate with God through prayer. Sometimes we make prayer out to be something that only the professionals can do. They use special words such as *thee* and *thou*; they wear special clothes and place their hands a particular way. You might be surprised to know that Jesus didn't pray like that. He didn't teach his disciples to pray like that.

In a conversation about prayer, Jesus said, "And when you come before God, don't turn that into a theatrical production either. All these people making a regular show out of their prayers, hoping for stardom! Do you think God sits in a box seat? Here's what I want you to do: Find a quiet, secluded place so you won't be tempted to role-play before God. Just be there as simply and honestly as you can manage. The focus will shift from you to God, and you will begin to sense his grace" (Matt. 6:5–6 Message).

Don't worry about the words you use, because God knows your heart. Don't worry about whether you're sitting or standing, because God wants to hear from you.

I have three kids I love dearly. When they want to speak to me, the important thing isn't the position of their hands or the formality of their words; it's the genuineness of their heart. That's true with God as well.

Decide to spend some time daily telling God what's happening in your life and what you are thinking and feeling. It will do more for your journey than you know.

I Decided to Learn about God Daily

I was never a reader before I became a Christian. If you aren't a person who reads much, that's okay. But people who grow in their relationship with God spend some time reading the Bible daily. Why? Because in the Bible, we learn things about God we never knew.

I have a box in my office at home with all the letters my wife wrote me while we were dating and she was away at college. I read and reread those letters because I wanted to know her better. The same is true with God. The stories we read in the Bible tell how God worked in the lives of people throughout history. What's amazing is that as you read those stories you learn that God wants to be faithful to you the same way he was faithful to them.

You don't have to read the entire book in one sitting! Just decide to carve out some time daily to spend with God. Think of it this way—if prayer is speaking to God, then spending time reading the Bible is God's opportunity to speak to you. I've learned that if there's something I'm praying about, often the answer can be found in the section of the Bible I'm reading that day.

I Went to Church Weekly

As I wanted to grow in my faith, I thought the best place to be would be around others who wanted to do the same. When I started to attend church, I sang songs from my heart to God. I opened the Bible, and I was taught how to walk with God through a gifted Bible teacher. I got to know some people who became friends with me and helped me along as I took my first few steps, and I could even use the talents God gave me to help others connect with him.

Getting involved in a church regularly is so important. I know we live in a very busy world, but if we don't make the time to cultivate our relationship with God, no one will do it for us. So we must protect our time and prioritize it. All these years later, I have never regretted that decision to go to church regularly.

I Found Some Friends on the Journey

I had many friends when I became a Christian and started to follow Jesus, but I knew that I also needed friends who would help me along in my spiritual journey. As I went to church and got to know people, friendships naturally formed, and I saw my spiritual life soar because of the people I got to know.

I have learned that getting involved in a small group helps tremendously, because there's nothing greater than going through a difficult time and knowing that you're not alone. It's comforting to know people are praying for me and are ready to help in whatever way possible when I have a problem. It makes life a little easier knowing you have a support system of people who love God and love you.

I Went Public with My Faith through Baptism

Baptism is a public symbol of the inward commitment you've made to follow Jesus. Baptism is a command of Jesus. He asks every one of his followers to be baptized in water. Why? Because in baptism we identify with Jesus's death when we go in the water and then identify with Jesus's resurrection when we emerge from the water (see Rom. 6).

When I was baptized, it was a big deal. It was one of the first times when I read something in the Bible that Jesus asked me to do and I obeyed. Baptism has so much rich meaning and depth, but on a practical level it set a pattern of obedience in my life where I wanted to do God's will.

I recognize these five decisions aren't the answer to all life's questions, but they have been a foundation in my life. They have helped me keep taking steps in God's direction. In the following chapters, I will explain each decision I made and give you some tools for growing in your faith.

One of my favorite movie quotations comes from *The Hurricane*, a film starring Denzel Washington about a boxer wrongfully convicted of murder. In the movie, Lesra Martin's character is in a bookstore and picks up a book by Washington's character. The book moves Martin to help

Reuben "The Hurricane" Carter get a fair trial and, ultimately, get out of prison. When he rhetorically asks his friends how a book can move a person to act, his friends respond, "Sometimes you pick the book; sometimes the book picks you."

Not only have you picked this book, but this book has also picked you because it contains the tools for spiritual growth that can serve you for a lifetime.

1

What Does It Mean to Be a Christian?

I received a very kind gift for my fourteenth birthday. A family friend gave me a gold chain that was so cool; it made me look like a member of *Miami Vice*. A gold necklace like that probably cost $500 in 1989 when it was given to me. I wore it to school thinking I was the coolest kid in the world. My classmates *oohed* and *aahed* over my recently acquired gold chain, and I internally vowed that I would never take it off.

That lasted for three days. As I left for school on the third day, I looked at myself in the mirror and noticed something—there was a discoloration on my neck. I thought I was turning into the Incredible Hulk because my neck was turning green. My fashionable gold chain had turned green as well because it wasn't gold. It was a fake! I was angry that I had been given a counterfeit rather than the real thing. I learned that not everything is real just because of its label.

So here's my question for you—what is a Christian? There are enough answers to go around. A 2009 Gallup poll showed that 78 percent of Americans consider themselves Christians.[1] An ABC News poll showed that 75 percent of Americans believe they will go to heaven when they die. Another 14 percent of those surveyed believe in heaven as well; they just aren't sure whether they'll get to go in.[2]

In my experience as a pastor, I have found that people give various reasons why they call themselves Christians:

"I'm a Christian because I'm an American."

"I'm a Christian because my parents believed."

"I was born a Christian and grew up in the church."

"I'm a Christian because I'm not Jewish or Muslim."

My problem with these answers is they don't mention the only reason a person is a Christian. Here's the challenge: You can go to church and not be a Christian. You can read the Bible and not be a Christian. You can eliminate bad habits, pray daily, and try to be a moral person and still not be a Christian. All these habits are good, and Christians should do them, but the actions alone don't make a person a believer.

What then is a Christian? A Christian is a person whom God has forgiven through the finished work of Jesus Christ on the cross. The Bible says:

> Once we, too, were foolish and disobedient. We were misled and became slaves to many lusts and pleasures. Our lives were full of evil and envy, and we hated each other. But— "When God our Savior revealed his kindness and love, he saved us, not because of the righteous things we had done, but because of his mercy. He washed away our sins, giving us a new birth and new life through the Holy Spirit. He generously poured out the Spirit upon us through Jesus Christ our Savior." (Titus 3:3–6)

We are Christians because of the finished work of Jesus on the cross. We are sinners who have fallen short of God's standard. God came to Earth in the person of Jesus and, being fully God and fully man, he died for us and paid the price for our sins. Through our faith in him, we receive forgiveness of our sins and the gift of eternal life.

In the Bible, a law-enforcement officer once asked the apostle Paul the most important question a person can ask: "What must I do to be saved?" Paul responded, "Believe in the Lord Jesus and you will be saved" (Acts 16:31).

Here's the point: being a Christian isn't about what you do; it's about what Jesus has done. He loves you. He died for you. He forgives you when you open your heart to believe.

So how do you know whether you are a Christian? The Bible says it's a good thing to test ourselves to make sure our faith is real. "Examine yourselves to see if your faith is genuine. Test yourselves. Surely you know that Jesus Christ is among you; if not, you have failed the test of genuine faith" (2 Cor. 13:5).

The apostle John was one of the original twelve disciples who followed Jesus. Toward the end of John's life, he wrote a letter to the church at large, letting them know how they can have eternal life and be confident and secure that they are truly Christians. He wrote at the end of 1 John, "I have written this to you who believe in the name of the Son of God, so that you may know you have eternal life" (5:13).

So what things did John write that can assure us we are Christians? We'll learn there are four tests to see whether we are Christians.

Test #1—Confess Jesus as Lord

> Whoever confesses that Jesus is the Son of God, God abides in him, and he in God. (1 John 4:15 NKJV)

The first mark of a true Christian is that he or she confesses that Jesus is Lord, which differs from simply believing in God. The Bible says that even demons believe in God and tremble (James 2:19). Confessing Jesus as Lord means calling on God to save you through the finished work of Jesus on the cross. The apostle Paul put it this way: "If you confess with your mouth the Lord Jesus and believe in your heart that God has raised Him from the dead, you will be saved. For with the heart one believes unto righteousness, and with the mouth confession is made unto salvation" (Rom. 10:9–10 NKJV).

Being a Christian has nothing to do with being a good person or your good deeds outweighing your bad deeds. All these lines of reasoning are variations of saying, "I'm good enough to save myself." The only problem is we can't save ourselves. We cannot deal with the fact that you and I are fallen, broken, sinful people, which is why the Bible tells us to confess with our mouth that Jesus is Lord and believe in our heart that God raised him from the dead. Understand these are not academic exercises. These two acts signify a paradigm shift in a person's life.

Confess with your mouth that Jesus is Lord, saying, "Jesus, you're in charge. You control my life. I resign that position to you. You're the master, and I'm the servant." Making Jesus Lord of your life is not about title; it's about control. It's about giving him the power to lead, direct, and guide you.

Believing in your heart that God raised Jesus from the dead is a statement declaring that, at the cross, my sins were paid for. When I place my trust in that fact—that Jesus is the only one who can save me—that's when the Bible says, "You are saved." We aren't saved because our parents were Christians or because we gave money to a charity last year. Jesus's death and resurrection are what saves us from a life of futility and misery and an eternity separated from God.

Some people think they're too bad and that God would never accept them. However, there's a promise in the Bible that says otherwise. Romans 10:13 tells us, "Whoever calls on the name of the LORD will be saved" (NKJV). It doesn't matter who you are or what you've done; salvation is about who Jesus is (he's God, and he has the power to forgive) and what Jesus has done (he died for us, rose again, and invites us to experience the life he offers us).

Test #2—Obey the Commands of God

> For this is the love of God, that we keep His command-ments. And His commandments are not burdensome. (1 John 5:3 NKJV)

A revelation happens when we're confronted with the commands of God. First, the commands of God show who God is because they show us God's heart toward us. His commands are given to us out of love and a sincere desire for us to live the best life possible. If you have kids (or if you were ever given rules by your parents), then you know your rules for your kids are based in love. You want your kids to be safe, loving, and functioning members of society, so you create boundaries that ensure they have the chance to grow into the best versions of themselves.

God's commands show God's love for us and his de-sire to lead us to live in a way that will take us into the abundant life he promised us. Jesus said, "I have come that they may have life, and that they may have it more abundantly" (John 10:10 NKJV). In short, obeying God's commands leads to the best possible life. In a world where most people simply exist and just "get by" with life, Jesus offers a life with depth, meaning, and purpose in him.

The second discovery we find in obeying the commands of God is the revelation of our faith. Our desire to obey God shows our relationship with him. True Christians won't be perfect in their obedience to God; however, they will seek to obey God. True Christians seek to guide their lives by what God says. This doesn't mean Christians never sin. Unfortunately, we are all sinners, and just because you've become a Christian doesn't mean you'll never sin again. However, true Christians will be miserable when they sin because they will know they are living apart from God's guidance.

The Bible says, "Those who have been born into God's family do not make a practice of sinning, because God's life is in them. So they can't keep on sinning, because they are children of God" (1 John 3:9). True followers of Jesus will feel uncomfortable when they sin because the Holy Spirit is working in their lives.

I became a Christian on May 29, 1993, in my brother's kitchen. He shared the gospel with me, and I responded by inviting Jesus Christ into my life to be Savior and Lord. However, the first thing I did after making the most important decision in my life was go to a baseball game.

I grew up in Boston, and I was there visiting my brother when I decided to follow Jesus. So I went to Fenway Park that evening with my girlfriend Carey (now my wife of sixteen years) and looked forward to enjoying the game.

Here's what you need to know about me: before becoming a Christian, I cussed like a sailor who spent all his free time watching *The Usual Suspects*. My language got especially salty when I watched sporting events.

So during the game, when the umpire made a call I didn't agree with, I stood and said, "Why you—" But somehow I stopped, looked around, and sat down. Carey looked at me, wondering what I would say. I turned to her and said, "I'm a Christian now, and I don't think God wants me to talk like that anymore." I had been a Christian for only three hours, and God was already working in my life.

Does this mean I've never said a word I've regretted since that day? Unfortunately, I have. But whenever it happened, I was unhappy about it, and thankfully God has given me victory in this area of my life. You don't enter a state of perfection when you become a Christian. Instead, you come to an awareness of sin, and the Holy Spirit works in your life to give you victory.

Test #3—Build Friendships with Believers

> Everyone who believes that Jesus is the Christ has become a child of God. And everyone who loves the Father loves his children, too. (1 John 5:1)

It's impossible to grow in your faith alone. Christianity was not designed to be practiced in solitude. The Christian faith works best when we are engaged with others in the journey. Jesus had twelve disciples with him almost everywhere he went. We must follow this model as well.

As a young Christian, I wanted to grow in my faith. I didn't know any other Christians, so I thought the best place to find others of like faith was church. It seemed simple enough, but I had never attended a church in my life. Here's what I found when I started to attend a church: I found people headed in the same direction I was—sincere people more than willing to help me in my new faith journey.

Early in my Christian walk, I met a man named Bill. He wasn't a Bible teacher or theologian. He lived three doors down from me and was a construction worker. He invited me to knock on his door whenever I had questions about the Bible. I kept a notebook of all the questions I had.

Once I had two pages of questions, I would knock on his door, and he would graciously spend hours with me answering every inquiry I had about the Scriptures. Those sessions gave me such confidence in God's Word and helped me build my life on God's truths. Godly men such as Bill and many others who befriended me and mentored me are some reasons I still walk with God.

Here's the bottom line: if you're a Christian, go to church. Get involved. Build some friendships with followers of Christ who inspire you with their faith. We'll cover this topic in-depth in chapter 3, but suffice it to say, this decision is one of the best you can make in your life.

Test #4—Grow in Your Love for Others

He who says he is in the light, and hates his brother, is in darkness until now. He who loves his brother abides in the light, and there is no cause for stumbling in him. But he who hates his brother is in darkness and walks in darkness, and does not know where he is going, because the darkness has blinded his eyes. (1 John 2:9–11 NKJV)

My five-year-old daughter, Mia, recently memorized the Bible passage on the fruit of the Spirit. It's a section in the Bible that talks about what it looks like when the Holy Spirit begins to work in our lives: "But the fruit of the Spirit is love, joy, peace, longsuffering, kindness, goodness, faithfulness, gentleness, self-control. Against such there is no law" (Gal. 5:22–23 NKJV).

I told her how important it is to hide God's Word in her heart and that God was pleased with her committing sections of the Bible to memory. Mia was so happy. Twenty minutes later, she got into an argument with her three-year-old brother and punched him. So I took her aside and asked, "Mia, is acting like that showing any of the fruit of the Spirit?" She agreed that her actions weren't loving and apologized to her brother.

This is what it looks like when we say we love God and hate our brother. When God transforms your life, you become a more loving person. God changes your heart and gives you compassion and grace for those you wouldn't have any time for previously.

Do you know why John is so passionate about this topic in particular? It's because John wasn't talking about this in theory. God had transformed his life from an angry, over-reacting hothead to a person of grace and love.

There's a scene in the Bible where Jesus comes to a town with his disciples, including John, who was a young man at the time. The townspeople aren't interested in Jesus's message of love and grace, and they ask him to leave. When they don't receive Jesus's message, John and his brother James say, "Do you want us to call down fire from heaven and consume them like Elijah did?" (see Luke 9:54). Essentially they were saying, "Lord, they won't receive the message of love, grace, and forgiveness. Do you want us to kill everyone?" This scene and many other encounters earned John and his brother the nickname *Boanerges*, which means "sons of thunder."

Let's fast-forward a few years. After the death and resurrection of Jesus, the same John who wanted to torch a town instead preached the gospel and saw the grace of God save a town. John's name was changed from "son of thunder" to "the apostle of love." How does this transformation happen? It happens when a person has a real encounter with the living God.

So, are you a Christian? The answer to that question comes down to what you've done with the gospel message that Jesus Christ lived a perfect life, died on a cross, and was buried. Three days later he rose from the dead and offers forgiveness and grace to every person who comes to him.

Have you invited Jesus Christ to come into your life and forgive you of your sins? If not, you can pray this prayer and ask God to forgive you because of what Jesus did. He loves you and wants to do great work in your life. So if you're ready, pray:

> Dear God, I open my heart and invite you in. I'm sorry for my sins. I turn from them and turn to you. Thank you for sending Jesus to die for me. I receive Jesus as my Savior and Lord. Thank you for saving me. In Jesus's name. Amen.

If you just prayed that prayer and meant it in faith, Jesus Christ has now taken residence in your heart and life! Your decision to follow Jesus means God has forgiven you. God has started to work in your life right now, and you will spend eternity in heaven.

But this isn't the finish line—it's just the starting point. This is the first step to building your life on God's truth. So now that you're a Christian, how do you communicate with God? What do you say? How do you know that God hears you? How do you know whether you're praying the right way? We'll pick up that topic next.

2

Learning to Pray

I remember the first time I prayed out loud in public. I had been a Christian for about four months, and I was in the Atlantic Ocean waiting to be baptized. The church leaders baptizing me asked whether I would pray before professing my faith in Jesus through water baptism.

I was scared to death, but twenty years later, I still remember the terrified prayer I prayed. "God, thanks for everything. I'm here to be baptized. I'm here . . . I'm here,

Lord . . . Amen!" Here's what's odd: I had never been nervous praying. I prayed to God throughout the day as someone would talk to a friend. However, when I got around two men whom I considered "spiritual," I froze and couldn't pray. I thought I needed to pepper my prayer with a "thee" and a "thou" to sound holy. I became very self-conscious over every word, and in the end I didn't say much.

This desire we have to impress others (or even impress God) with our prayers is the start of the problem. When we try to impress or sound holy, we miss the point of prayer, which is simply connecting with God. Some people think that the length of your prayers is what makes your time with God special. Here's what I've noted: every recorded prayer of Jesus can be recited in less than two minutes. So if it's not the vernacular of the prayer or the duration of the prayer, what is the key to effective prayer?

Jesus's disciples came to him one day and asked him an important question. They wanted to learn to pray.

> Now it came to pass, as He was praying in a certain place, when He ceased, that one of His disciples said to Him, "Lord, teach us to pray, as John also taught his disciples." (Luke 11:1 NKJV)

These disciples didn't ask Jesus to teach them to do miracles, to preach, or to walk on water. Instead, they asked him to instruct them in how to connect with the Father in prayer the same way he did. This question didn't surprise Jesus. In ancient Jewish culture, a disciple wanted to learn to do everything like his rabbi, his teacher. True to form, these first-century disciples were seeking to learn the best way to connect with God, which would be the way their rabbi prayed.

Jesus's response to their inquiry is the fifty-nine words we call the Lord's Prayer. It should more adequately be called the Disciples' Prayer because Jesus taught them to pray this prayer. I don't believe Jesus is teaching them that this is the only prayer they should pray. Instead, I believe this prayer is a template for us on how to connect with God in prayer.

Now it came to pass, as He was praying in a certain place, when He ceased, that one of His disciples said to Him, "Lord, teach us to pray, as John also taught his disciples." So He said to them, "When you pray, say:

Our Father in heaven, hallowed be Your name. Your kingdom come. Your will be done on earth as it is in heaven. Give us day by day our daily bread. And forgive us our sins, for we also forgive everyone who is indebted to us.

And do not lead us into temptation, but deliver us from
the evil one." (Luke 11:1–4 NKJV)

Jesus dispelled the myth that answered prayers have to
do with the words you use and the length of your prayer.
Jesus's prayer is short but potent. I love that what Jesus
taught his disciples was countercultural in that day. Rabbis
in the first century usually taught the opposite. One famous
rabbi wrote, "Whoever is long in prayer is heard." Another
said, "Whenever the righteous make their prayer long,
their prayer is heard."[3] Jesus focuses on the relationship
and the content of the prayer rather than the duration. Yet
in this model prayer, Jesus shows us five keys to effective
prayer that we can apply to our prayers and know that we
pray in the way Jesus taught us.

Our Holy Father

The Jews addressed God by calling him Lord out of rev-
erence. Their respect of God was so extreme that they
wouldn't even utter God's name. Yet, when Jesus died for
us, he brought us back into relationship with God, and
this prayer shows us the relationship we have with him is
a Father-child relationship. Why did Jesus instruct us to

address God as "our Father"? Because God is not some distant being who's unapproachable and disengaged from our lives. So when we pray, we're reminded that God loves us as a father loves his kids.

When Jesus adds the second phrase of his introduction to this model prayer, he says, "Hallowed be Your name." The word *hallowed* simply means "holy." It shows us that God is separate from humankind. He is good and perfect in all his ways. Jesus wants us to remember this truth because God has our best interests at heart. Even when God doesn't answer our prayers exactly the way we ask, we can be confident that our heavenly Father loves us and always works toward what is in our best interest.

God's Kingdom and God's Will

When I started college, my dad decided to buy me a car. He told me to check out some used cars and find one I really liked. He said the next day he would come with me and we'd buy it. So I went to a few places and browsed the inventory. That's when I saw the perfect vehicle for me. It was a purple lowrider pickup truck. I loved it. It had more than one hundred thousand miles on it, but that didn't matter. All I could picture was my driving it down the road, blasting some music out of it because in the back it had state-of-the-art speakers . . . roughly the size of a coffin.

I took my dad to see it the next day, and he had a much different perspective than I did. He showed me the giant crack in the windshield, the dents all over the truck, and that one door didn't open. I didn't buy the truck. Once I saw things from his perspective, it changed my desire.

The same thing is true with prayer. When Jesus prays, "Your kingdom come. Your will be done on earth as it is in heaven," it's a powerful statement. In heaven, everything happens exactly the way God wants it to. This is God's desire for the earth as a whole and for our lives specifically. This should be our ambition as well. We should seek to live so that God's will is evident in our lives.

> For I know the thoughts that I think toward you, says the LORD, thoughts of peace and not of evil, to give you a future and a hope. (Jer. 29:11 NKJV)

God's will is to give you a future and a hope. His desire is to give you a life filled with purpose, meaning, and significance. That doesn't mean life will be easy, but it does mean it will be worth it. I want you to notice something: Jesus doesn't teach us to stack our laundry list of requests up front. Instead, he instructs us to realize to whom we're praying—the God of the universe who loves us and wants us to call him Father. Then, once we've acknowledged his holiness, we can bring God our requests.

Daily Bread

Baking bread in the ancient Middle East was a daily activity. Bread was a staple item, and you baked it every day to feed your family. When Jesus teaches us to ask, "Give us this day our daily bread," it's a petition for God's provision in our lives. To this day, I am still blown away that the God of the universe cares about my needs and desires.

> When I look at the night sky and see the work of
> your fingers—
> the moon and the stars you set in place—
> what are mere mortals that you should think
> about them,
> human beings that you should care for them?
> (Ps. 8:3–4)

Another important point to note is that "Give us this day our daily bread" is a reminder that everything we have comes from God. He is our ultimate provider. He gives us the air we breathe, the skills to function in our career, and the resources to purchase life's necessities. It's freeing to realize that I am not the source of everything I need. My loving heavenly Father is the source of everything, and he is willing to provide for me. We can come to him with any request, knowing that he will always answer. He might not answer in the exact way we hope, but he will answer and meet our needs.

> Whatever is good and perfect comes down to us from God our Father, who created all the lights in the heavens. (James 1:17)

On Forgiving and Being Forgiven

John, a pastor on my staff, recently loaned his car to a member of our church. However, the member dented his car while driving it back to our office. I heard about the incident, and I asked John what he would do about this.

John said, "I forgave him and told him not to worry about it." I was angry. I told John that this person was irresponsible and that the only way he would learn was if he had to pay for his infraction. John smiled and said, "Bob, the problem is that I borrowed my friend's truck a few weeks ago and I dented it while I was using it, and he forgave me."

I felt a bit foolish. However, I was also reminded of an important lesson on the power of forgiveness. Jesus taught us in the model prayer to say, "And forgive us our sins, for we also forgive everyone who is indebted to us" (Luke 11:4). We can come to God because of forgiveness. When we place our faith in Jesus, we receive his forgiveness for all our sins and trespasses, meaning we have no right to withhold forgiveness from others. Regardless of what someone has done to us, we owed a greater debt to God that was forgiven through Jesus. Forgiveness is difficult because it's not the natural response when we're hurt. Our natural response is revenge because we want the person who hurt us to feel the same pain we feel.

In the Gospels, there's a story in which Jesus has dinner with a religious leader, and as they eat, a woman comes in and pours oil on Jesus's feet. She weeps on his feet and dries the tears with her hair. It's a powerful picture because this woman was a prostitute; in that culture, she was a sinner of the worst kind.

The religious leader thought, "If Jesus were a prophet, he wouldn't even allow this woman to touch him." Jesus then told the man a story that shows his heart and demonstrates to us the true meaning of forgiveness.

> "A man loaned money to two people—500 pieces of silver to one and 50 pieces to the other. But neither of them could repay him, so he kindly forgave them both, canceling their debts. Who do you suppose loved him more after that?"
>
> Simon answered, "I suppose the one for whom he canceled the larger debt."
>
> "That's right," Jesus said. Then he turned to the woman and said to Simon, "Look at this woman kneeling here. When I entered your home, you didn't offer me water to wash the dust from my feet, but she has washed them with her tears and wiped them with her hair. You didn't greet me with a kiss, but from the time I first came in, she has not stopped kissing my feet. You neglected the courtesy of olive oil to anoint my head, but she has anointed my feet with rare perfume.
>
> "I tell you, her sins—and they are many—have been forgiven, so she has shown me much love. But a person who is forgiven little shows only little love." (Luke 7:41–47)

If you're a Christian, then you're like that woman. We have been forgiven so much, and therefore we must model forgiveness to others. This is why we pray and thank God for forgiving us, because it makes forgiving others easier.

There's also another reason we need to forgive—because it's the best way to live. When I choose not to forgive, I am trapped in a prison of anger and bitterness. The only way to be released from this prison is to forgive. It's the key to opening the cell and living in freedom.

We don't forgive because we believe we're letting that person who hurt us off the hook. Forgiveness is the way for us to keep the past from controlling us. We all know people who have been hurt by an experience or relationship, and to this day that pain controls their lives because of their refusal to forgive. Forgiveness is the medicine that keeps us from becoming bitter people.

> Get rid of all bitterness, rage and anger, brawling and slander, along with every form of malice. Be kind and compassionate to one another, forgiving each other, just as in Christ God forgave you. (Eph. 4:31–32 NIV)

Dealing with Temptation

Jesus closes his model prayer by teaching us to recognize our propensity for sin. We are by nature fallen people, and we need God's power in our lives to avoid the temptation that will hurt us. We should note that when Jesus teaches us to pray, "And do not lead us into temptation, but deliver us from the evil one" (Luke 11:4), he is not saying that God marches us into temptation and then drops us off. Instead, this prayer, as one New Testament paraphrase states, "Keep[s] us clear of temptation."[4]

> Let no one say when he is tempted, "I am tempted by God"; for God cannot be tempted by evil, nor does He Himself tempt anyone. But each one is tempted when he is drawn away by his own desires and enticed. Then, when desire has conceived, it gives birth to sin; and sin, when it is full-grown, brings forth death. (James 1:13–15 NKJV)

Jesus teaches us to ask God to lead us in a way that we won't be sidetracked and caught by temptation.

We should understand that temptation by itself is not sin. We read in the Gospels that even Jesus was tempted. He never gave in to it, but he was tempted. When you and I are tempted, it's our opportunity to draw close to God, ask for his help and strength, and resist temptation.

> The temptations in your life are no different from what others experience. And God is faithful. He will not allow the temptation to be more than you can stand. When you are tempted, he will show you a way out so that you can endure. (1 Cor. 10:13)

Asking for God's help in temptation is an honest admission of our vulnerabilities. None of us is resistant to temptation. We all struggle. The more honest we are with God, the more open we are to following his lead as we navigate temptation.

The beauty of prayer is that you don't need a theology degree to pray correctly. You can simply talk to God and converse with him throughout your day. You don't have to kneel or light a candle to talk to God. The Bible says, "Pray without ceasing" (1 Thess. 5:17 NKJV). This doesn't mean you must quit your job and pray twenty-four hours a day. It simply means your life has an attitude of prayer. The words don't have to be eloquent. God simply wants to hear from you.

3

The Importance of Community

*I*n Atlanta, there's a cool mall called Underground Atlanta. Well, at least it was cool in 1993 when my band was on tour and we stopped in Atlanta for the day. As we walked into the mall, we noticed the most peculiar street musician.

Most street performers play one instrument and do their best to play well enough to earn the random change of the local passerby. However, this mall minstrel played three instruments simultaneously. He played the drums with his feet, guitar with his hands, and harmonica with his mouth, plus he sang at the top of his lungs. It was a sight. I couldn't get the image of this man struggling to play every instrument by himself out of my mind. I thought how much better his music would be and how much more fun he would have if he joined a band.

God's Hit Song

Much like music, life has a rhythm and pattern to it. The first two chapters of the Bible are written in the pattern of poetry and song to help memorization and to emphasize a point. Follow the flow of Moses as he teaches us the creation song . . .

Day 1—God creates the world and creates light, and it was good.

Day 2—God separates the waters and gives the sky its name, and it was good.

Day 3—God separates land and creates trees, seeds, and plants, and it was good. (Day 3 is a crescendo in the song because God says it is good twice. It's notable that this is the reason most weddings in Israel occur on Tuesday, because God said "it was good" twice on the third day.)

Day 4—God creates the sun, moon, and stars, and it was good.

Day 5—God creates sea life and birds, and it was good.

Day 6—God creates man. Here's where there's a bad note played in the song. Genesis 1 is the overview of creation, but Genesis 2 zeros in on God's final creation—man. It's here we find a problem in the song that's sung. Everything until now has been good, and the rhythm of God's song is flowing. Then the disc begins to skip, and we hear there's a note out of key . . .

And the LORD God said, "It is not good that man should be alone; I will make him a helper comparable to him." (Gen. 2:18 NKJV)

What is it that causes the song of creation to go out of key? Loneliness. The man being alone is what God says isn't good. When God sees that it isn't good for Adam to be alone, he creates Eve to be his companion. Once they are united, the song of creation is complete.

Joining a Band

As a new believer, I learned that I couldn't walk with God and grow in my relationship with God by myself. The Christian life is impossible to live alone. We were created to live in community with others and to do life with fellow believers headed in the same direction.

As a young musician, I practiced alone in my bedroom and learned a few songs in my first months of playing. However, when I started to play with a drummer who lived across the street and a guitar player who lived a block away, my playing improved exponentially.

People ask why this happens. Musicians improve most by playing with other musicians because that's how instruments are meant to be played—in concert with other instruments. This is how we grow best as Christians as well—when we're in concert with other Christians.

Even though God's song warns us "it isn't good for man to be alone," people are lonelier than ever. Robert Putnam, author of the bestselling book *Bowling Alone*, notes that more people than ever are bowling. However, memberships in bowling leagues are in rapid decline. His point is that more people than ever are bowling alone. It's tragic that we live in the most connected period of human history, and yet we're lonelier than ever.

We have smart phones with phone, video, and texting capabilities. We have social media websites where we can learn what everyone is eating, thinking, and doing at any moment. Technology has given us everything except telepathy when it comes to communication ability. Despite this, many people have a deeply rooted sense of loneliness. A Christian doesn't have to feel this isolation. Followers of Jesus can not only feel the presence of God in their lives but also live in community with other believers.

The Greek word *koinonia*, which our English Bibles translate as "fellowship," is a robust word rich in meaning. Christians sometimes think of fellowship as hanging out with friends and eating. *Koinonia* does mean hanging out together, but it also has a deeper sense of oneness, unity of purpose, and a common direction. It means communion and caring for one another in the highs and lows of life. The first church, the church built by the original disciples of Jesus, focused on *koinonia* and experienced the blessed life God intended for us.

> All the believers devoted themselves to the apostles' teaching, and to fellowship, and to sharing in meals (including the Lord's Supper), and to prayer. (Acts 2:42)

One of my favorite movies is the first *Lord of the Rings* film. I love the scene in which Frodo decides that the ring must be taken back to Mordor and destroyed. He stands and says that he will take the ring to Mordor, and at that moment the nine companions come together as "The Fellowship of the Ring." They unite in a common goal, purpose, and mission.

This is an example of our lives as Christians. We have fellowship with God and with the Lord Jesus, and because of that we have fellowship with one another.

> That which we have seen and heard we declare to you, that you also may have fellowship with us; and truly our fellowship is with the Father and with His Son Jesus Christ. (1 John 1:3 NKJV)

So, what does fellowship look like practically? In ancient Jewish culture, fellowship was essential to life. The greatest joys and darkest moments were never to be embraced alone. For example, the book of Job tells about the worst moments of Job's life. He had lost nearly everything dear to him, and he sat alone, trying to cope with these tragedies. At that moment, his three closest friends arrived to bear the pain with him.

Now when Job's three friends heard of all this adversity that had come upon him, each one came from his own place—Eliphaz the Temanite, Bildad the Shuhite, and Zophar the Naamathite. For they had made an appointment together to come and mourn with him, and to comfort him. And when they raised their eyes from afar, and did not recognize him, they lifted their voices and wept; and each one tore his robe and sprinkled dust on his head toward heaven. So they sat down with him on the ground seven days and seven nights, and no one spoke a word to him, for they saw that his grief was very great. (Job 2:11–13 NKJV)

This scene describes an ancient Hebrew custom called "sitting Shiva." *Shiva* is a derivative of the number seven in Hebrew, and it is something close friends do when someone loses a loved one. They get together to sit, weep, and be there. No words are spoken for seven days.

Job had lost his children, his health, and his business. (His life had all the makings of a country and western song.) The fellowship of his friends helped him deal with the most difficult season of his life.

In the other extreme, when something great happens in your life, you want someone to rejoice with you. A few years ago, I was playing golf at a par-three course near my office, and I hit a hole in one. The hole was only eighty yards, but when I walked on the green and found the ball in the cup, I felt as if I had won the Masters. There was just one problem—I was alone. There was no one there with whom to celebrate the moment. It was just me, excited beyond belief—but alone.

> Or suppose a woman has ten silver coins and loses one. Doesn't she light a lamp, sweep the house and search carefully until she finds it? And when she finds it, she calls her friends and neighbors together and says, "Rejoice with me; I have found my lost coin." (Luke 15:8–9 NIV)

In this parable, Jesus talks about finding lost things. He notes that we are wired to celebrate. We want to share our joy with others. These ten coins were likely this woman's dowry. In this culture, the dowry was the only money she brought into the marriage, and the coins (each worth about a day's wages) were technically hers, even if the marriage was dissolved.

The fact that her dowry was only ten coins shows that she wasn't a person of great financial means. So when she found this coin, it was not only a great relief but also a reason to celebrate. How sad would it have been if she had no one with whom to celebrate this moment?

Rejoice with those who rejoice; mourn with those who mourn. (Rom. 12:15 NIV)

God has established a place and a group where, in the best and worst times of your life, you can feel love, comfort, and acceptance—the church. God established the church so we can grow in God's Word and grow with God's people. More than fifty references in the New Testament use the phrase "one another." Here are a few:

Love one another. (John 13:34)

Serve one another. (Gal. 5:13)

Accept one another. (Rom. 15:7)

Encourage one another. (1 Thess. 5:11)

Bear one another's burdens. (Gal. 6:2)

Be kind to one another. (Eph. 4:32)

Forgive one another. (Col. 3:13)

Exhort one another. (Heb. 3:13)

My encouragement to you is don't just attend church. Get involved in your church. Serve in some capacity. Attend small group gatherings. Participate in classes. It's in doing these things that you'll meet people who will influence your life greatly and help you go to the next level in your relationship with God.

A few years ago when I was speaking at a conference, I ran into a couple I hadn't seen in years. They had attended the small group Bible study my wife and I had hosted in our home nearly fifteen years earlier. The couple had been dating at the time they attended our group, and now they were happily married with two beautiful children.

I told them how proud I was of them, and they said to me, "We want you to know that you're part of this. We remember leaving your little apartment every week and knowing that there were people who loved us and were helping us grow. We're married because you helped us understand God's love and how we're supposed to love each other." I walked away a little teary eyed, but my heart was bursting because another couple had learned that life is so much better when you aren't in a one-man band.

4

Studying the Bible

One night early in my marriage, I decided to cook dinner for my wife. Being the considerate husband I am, I chose to prepare my favorite meal—steak with white rice and black beans (a Cuban favorite). I didn't know how to make black beans, so I decided to call my mom and get some direction. She gave me detailed instructions over the phone, and before I hung up, she asked, "Robert, did you write all of that down?"

I said, "No, but I memorized it."

Armed with all the information I needed, I made a paste called *sofrito*, which is essential for good black beans. Then, after soaking the beans, I put everything in the pressure cooker and turned on *Indiana Jones and the Temple of Doom*.

Pressure cookers make this distinct sound as steam releases from the top. My mom said that after the pressure cooker stops making that sound for fifteen minutes, my beans would be done. So I'm watching *Indiana Jones*, and at the same time the creepy witch doctor rips a guy's heart out with his bare hands, I hear a boom in my kitchen that scares me half to death. What happened? My pressure cooker had exploded and scattered my beans all over the walls, behind the refrigerator, and even on the ceiling.

It turns out that my mom said to leave the beans in the pressure cooker for only fifteen minutes, and then get the beans out. Our apartment smelled like burned beans for the next three days. The good news is that my wife released me from all kitchen duties after that incident. Now when I decide to cook, I order pizza.

When it comes to physical food, there's nothing wrong with being all thumbs in the kitchen. However, when it comes to spiritual food, we all need to learn the keys to feeding ourselves with a healthy spiritual diet. If you want to grow spiritually and mature in your faith, you must learn how to feed on God's Word yourself. This is not to say that attending church services, listening to pastors, or reading books isn't important; those are all very important activities. However, all those things should be coupled with the daily activity of studying God's Word. Spiritual growth occurs in the daily reading of the Bible.

> People do not live by bread alone, but by every word that comes from the mouth of God. (Matt. 4:4)

Many Christians starve themselves all week until they get to church, then hope that one biblical message will sustain them and grow them in their faith. Imagine if a person did that physically. No one starves himself or herself all week and then gorges on one meal on Sunday. I would rather you eat a healthy diet of Scripture all week and then have a fine dining experience when you hear a pastor teach the Bible on Sunday.

Before I teach you the simple Bible study methods I have used for more than twenty years, I want you to make three decisions that will affect your spiritual maturity and your approach to the Bible.

Accept the Bible as Your Authority

Three years ago, my wife and I bought a dresser for our bedroom. I brought the box home and did what every man does: I disregarded the instructions because I believed I knew what I was doing. The result was a disaster. I nearly broke the dresser and hurt myself in the process. It was only when I humbled myself and accepted IKEA's instructions as my authority to build the dresser that the furniture turned out the way it was intended.

This is the story of many people's lives. We try to build our lives alone and end up making poor decisions that hurt our future, which is why we must agree that the Bible is our authority if we are to grow to spiritual maturity. The Bible serves us in many ways, but one is showing us God's way to live.

> The instructions of the Lord are perfect, reviving the soul. The decrees of the Lord are trustworthy, making wise the simple. The commandments of the Lord are right, bringing joy to the heart. The commands of the Lord are clear, giving insight for living. (Ps. 19:7–8)

Understand the Goal of Bible Study

Famed evangelist D. L. Moody wrote, "The Bible was not given to increase our knowledge but to change our lives." Before reading the Bible, I had many beliefs about God that weren't true. I thought God was angry with me. I believed that God was just waiting for me to mess up so he could ruin my life. However, when I started to read the Bible as a young Christian, I found that all those ideas were false. In fact, I learned that the opposite was true.

> I have loved you, my people, with an everlasting love. With unfailing love I have drawn you to myself. (Jer. 31:3)

> How precious are your thoughts about me, O God. They cannot be numbered! I can't even count them; they out-number the grains of sand! (Ps. 139:17–18)

> Again, the Kingdom of Heaven is like a merchant on the lookout for choice pearls. When he discovered a pearl of great value, he sold everything he owned and bought it! (Matt. 13:45–46)

These verses don't sound like someone who's angry with me but someone who's in love with me. Do you know that humanity (you and me) is the most important thing in all creation to God? God saw our fallen, sinful condition and didn't leave us there. Instead, he acted. He sent his Son to die for us, proving that he loves us passionately. The point is that the Bible teaches us what's true about God, and if we take the time to study God's Word, then we won't live with false ideas about God.

Decide That Spiritual Growth Matters

If you want to grow spiritually, you must take responsibility for your growth. Too many Christians waste time blaming others for the fact that they aren't growing. Spiritual growth begins with a personal decision to grow in your faith.

> Do not waste time arguing over godless ideas and old wives' tales. Instead, *train yourself* to be godly. (1 Tim. 4:7, emphasis added)

You are responsible to God for your growth as a Christian. The good news is that the church exists to assist, train, and encourage you, but you're ultimately responsible. This is important, because if you don't assume responsibility, you will never reach maturity. This is why getting into God's Word and studying for your own spiritual development is so important. It's a mark of a person who's serious about the things of God.

> Now the Berean Jews were of more noble character than those in Thessalonica, for they received the message with great eagerness and *examined the Scriptures every day* to see if what Paul said was true. (Acts 17:11 NIV, emphasis added)

How do you study the Bible? How do you take an ancient book and relate it to modern day? Scholars have developed a variety of study methods, but they are all based on three components:

Read it.

Meditate on it.

Live it.

Every style of Bible study teaches you to do these three things in different forms. My goal here is to teach you how to start reading the Bible for personal growth.

Step 1—Read It

This step sounds simple, but it involves answering one of the most frequently asked questions I get: "What version of the Bible should I read?" I answer this question in chapter 6, but I will add some thoughts here on which version of the Bible to use.

My conviction is that you should read the version of the Bible that your pastor reads from on Sunday. This way, as he teaches you the Bible, you can follow along word for word. I recommend this to the people at Calvary, the church I pastor. I teach from the New King James Version (NKJV) of the Bible. I like the New King James because it is a word-for-word translation of the original Greek and Hebrew. This translation has been updated from the original King James Version, thus removing all the "thees" and "thous," which aren't used in our common vernacular.

Having said that, I believe the best translation to use is the one you will read and understand. If you find the NKJV difficult to read, then I suggest the New Living Translation. This translation is written in conversational language that nearly everyone can understand and enjoy.

When you're reading the Bible, don't just read it as you'd read the newspaper. Read the Scriptures with a prayerful heart. Take a moment before you begin Bible reading to ask God to open your eyes to the wonders it contains. Never underestimate the power of asking God to open your eyes to his Word. God wants to reveal truth to you. Align your heart with his by praying and asking God to fill you with his Spirit, to give you a heart that's open to his Word, and to give you ears ready to hear his voice.

> Open my eyes that I may see wonderful things in your law. (Ps. 119:18 NIV)

Here is a simple prayer to pray before opening the Bible:

> God, open my eyes to what you want to say to me. I want to be open and teachable. I want you to teach me. In Jesus's name. Amen.

Step 2—Meditate on It

Meditation doesn't mean getting in the lotus position, chanting "om," and contemplating the universe. Meditation in the Bible means seriously and constantly thinking about a subject.

> Blessed is the one
>> who does not walk in step with the wicked
> or stand in the way that sinners take
>> or sit in the company of mockers,
> but whose delight is in the law of the LORD,
>> and who meditates on his law day and night.
>> (Ps. 1:1–2 NIV)

Notice how the Bible tells us to meditate on the words of God—day and night. I'll go out on a limb and say you've worried about something in your life. You played the scene repeatedly in your mind. You pondered every outcome and scenario. You imagined the conversations that would ensue and the responses people would have. Here's the good news: if you know how to worry, then you know how to meditate. Worry is simply a negative form of meditation.

When the Bible talks about meditating, the idea is like a cow chewing its cud. A cow doesn't simply eat grass. The cow eats it, and then the gastric juices start to work on it. Then the cow essentially vomits the grass and chews on it more, squeezing out every ounce of nutrients before finally digesting it. Essentially, meditation is thought digestion. I meditate on Scripture in four ways.

1. Imagine Being There

When you meditate on Scripture, imagine what it must have looked like, smelled like, and felt like. When I read Exodus, I like to picture in my mind what it must have been like to cross the Red Sea. When I read Joshua, I try to picture in my mind how amazing it must have been to see the walls of Jericho fall. This is one reason I recommend that Christians visit Israel; it changes your perspective because you can picture the stories in your mind in detail.

2. Repeat the Passage

I learned this approach from the book *Rick Warren's Bible Study Methods*. Repeating a passage and emphasizing a different word is great when you seek to memorize a truth from the Bible. Here is how Rick teaches us to use repetition to meditate on Scripture:

> Read through a verse aloud several times, each time emphasizing a different word, and watch new meanings develop. For instance, if you are meditating on Philippians 4:13, you would emphasize the words as follows:
>
> "*I* can do everything through him who gives me strength."
>
> "I *CAN* do everything through him who gives me strength."

"I can **DO** everything through him who gives me strength."

"I can do **EVERYTHING** through him who gives me strength."

"I can do everything **THROUGH** him who gives me strength."

"I can do everything through **HIM** who gives me strength."

"I can do everything through him **WHO** gives me strength."

"I can do everything through him who **GIVES** me strength."

"I can do everything through him who gives **ME** strength."

"I can do everything through him who gives me **STRENGTH**."

You will get 10 different meanings from this verse as you go through and emphasize a different word each time.[5]

3. Personalize the Bible

In this step, you insert your name in the passage and personalize it, making the Bible more personal. I have found that it grips me when I realize all God has done for me. For example, Ephesians 2:8–9 can be personalized as follows:

For by grace Bob has been saved through faith, and that not of yourselves; it is the gift of God, not of works, lest anyone should boast.

Obviously, this has its limits and doesn't work with any passage of the Bible. Changing Genesis 1:1 to say, "In the beginning, Bob created the heavens and the earth" doesn't work. However, when we can personalize the Bible, it's powerful and causes us to hide more of God's Word in our hearts.

4. Turn the Passage into a Prayer

Another way to meditate on Scripture is to turn the passage into the form of a prayer. So when the Bible states, "Do everything without complaining and arguing" (Phil. 2:14), turn that into a prayer. Pray something like, "Lord, help me to do all things without complaining. Give me the self-control to do what you've called me to without arguing. I want to represent you well. So I ask that when I open my mouth today, there won't even be a hint of complaining or arguing."

Meditating on Scripture is important because God promises to make the person who meditates on his Word live abundantly.

This Book of the Law shall not depart from your mouth, but you shall meditate in it day and night, that you may observe to do according to all that is written in it. For then you will make your way prosperous, and then you will have good success. (Josh. 1:8 NKJV)

Step 3—Live It

Applying what the Bible says to your life is where the rubber meets the road. There's a saying that we only believe the parts of the Bible that we actually do. As Christians, our job is to listen to God and obey his voice. The primary way God will speak to you will be through the Bible.

We need to read the Bible because it's how we learn about God's character and nature, but it's also how we learn to trust God. We watch as God leads the characters in the Bible, and we realize that God is doing the same thing in our lives. He leads us to live the best life possible. Be careful of simply taking the direction of God "under advisement," allowing God to be one of many counselors in life. Jesus taught us to hear the words of God and act on them. "If you know these things, blessed are you if you do them" (John 13:17 NKJV).

Storing information in your brain doesn't change your life. Having knowledge that you put into practice, on the other hand, makes all the difference.

When Jesus gave his most famous sermon, the Sermon on the Mount, he challenged his hearers not to simply listen to the message as an intellectual exercise. Instead, he warned those who gathered to take his words and put them to immediate use.

> Therefore whoever hears these sayings of Mine, and does them, I will liken him to a wise man who built his house on the rock: and the rain descended, the floods came, and the winds blew and beat on that house; and it did not fall, for it was founded on the rock.
>
> But everyone who hears these sayings of Mine, and does not do them, will be like a foolish man who built his house on the sand: and the rain descended, the floods came, and the winds blew and beat on that house; and it fell. And great was its fall. (Matt. 7:24–27 NKJV)

The point Jesus makes is that rain, wind, and floods come into everyone's life. There are no exceptions. We all experience difficult seasons in life. What makes a difference is what we do with God's Word.

If we listen to his words and do nothing with them, we're like people who build their house on sand and are blown away when the storms of life come. It's like the story of the three little pigs. Only the pig that built his house with something sturdy could withstand the attack of the big bad wolf. In the same way, if we apply the words of Jesus to our lives and build our house on the rock, the storms will still come, but we will still be standing once they have passed by.

Let me give you the equation I regularly teach my church about the importance of applying the Bible to our lives:

Information + Application = Transformation

I live in South Florida, so hurricanes are a reality in my life. I remember visiting the town of Homestead a few days before Hurricane Andrew hit that area in 1992. My friends and I were inside a vintage guitar shop looking for a good deal. The store was closing when we got there, so we decided to come back the next week.

When we tried to revisit the guitar store, it was impossible to reach it because of the level of devastation. Seeing the effects of that storm left an indelible impression on me. I no longer think of storms in the abstract. Instead, I see homes destroyed, cars demolished, and buildings leveled.

I see the same thing in people's lives. When the storms of life come and people have not built their lives on God's Word, the devastation is much the same—broken homes, fractured families, shattered dreams. I can't promise you that being a Christian means you'll never experience any problems in your life. What I can tell you is what Jesus promised. If you build your life on God's Word, when the storms of life hit, you'll still be standing when they're over.

5

Obedience through Baptism

*P*eople have weird tastes, especially when it comes to food. Some friends took me to a restaurant in Coral Gables, Florida. Even though the restaurant's concept of Latin and American fusion was creative, nothing sounded remotely appetizing. I wasn't too excited about it, but once I got the dish I ordered, it was amazing. I knew I had chosen wisely because out of all the dishes I sampled, the only dish I loved was the one I ordered.

I don't know whether you've ever felt that way in a restaurant—as if you somehow dodged a bullet. Although everything else I tried was good, it wasn't what I'd want to spend my evening eating. That's what makes people individuals. We all have different tastes and likes. For example, my wife loves the taste of Coke and milk mixed. I've tried counseling, therapy, and interventions, but she still loves it. I think it's just plain nasty! I'm not immune to the weird factor, either. I know it sounds disgusting, but I like the taste of cough medicine. When I get sick, cherry-flavored Robitussin is all I need. Most people gag when they have to take cough medicine. I, on the other hand, have been known to chug it straight from the bottle on occasion.

I'm always interested in other people's tastes for varieties of life. I don't understand how people can pay money to watch a tragic movie. Some of us need only to get out of bed in the morning to experience that for free. If you want me never to see a movie, just say the words, "It's really sad." Case closed. This bird has flown. I'm done. If it doesn't have explosions, funny dialogue, or an epic adventure, count me out.

Four Weddings and a Funeral

In light of that, there's one weird thing about me that few people understand: I like funerals. I know that sounds morbid, because most people don't like them. Now, let me clarify before you label me a mental case. I like to officiate funerals. I don't like it when people I love die, and I don't look forward to being the name on the program at my own memorial service. Yet, as a pastor, two of my "extracurricular" activities are weddings and funerals.

All pastors have a preference about which they would rather do. The problem is, I've never met anyone who likes funerals more than weddings . . . except me. So the question you're probably asking is, "Why?" I'll explain by asking you a question: What do you remember the pastor saying at the last wedding you attended, aside from the usual "I do" stuff? Don't remember? That is precisely my point. The pastor could read the phone book, and most of us would never know the difference, because no one cares what the pastor says at weddings.

At a funeral, we hang on every word because we look for God in those dark times. Sometimes, a simple Bible verse can be the difference between hope and despair. I like the role I play in funerals better because I think I make a difference.

Now, don't get me wrong; I don't like the sad part of funerals. I hate that part. I hate seeing people cry and saying good-bye to someone they love. It kills me inside. But

I love that people are open to God in those moments. It shows us that we aren't immortal, that we will see our Maker someday.

To clarify, I don't really hate weddings. I love the joy, the commitments made, and so forth. I appreciate the families (even the crazy ones) who want everything just perfect for this most special of days. But I wish I could fuse the joy of weddings with the sobriety of funerals.

The Water Boy

Is there ever a time when both death and commitment are celebrated? That's where baptism comes in. If you're like I was, you might have a mixed-up view of what baptism is because of your background or the church in which you grew up. In my childhood tradition, baptism was something done to infants so they could become part of a religion and to ensure they would go to heaven. Yet, when I became a Christian, I soon discovered that isn't exactly what the Bible teaches.

What I want us to experience together is one of the most important events in history. It's a baptism service that took place at the Jordan River two thousand years ago. This baptism had nothing to do with religion or a ritual.

Instead, it shows us what baptism really is—the mark of a life committed to God. That's why any Christian should want to be baptized.

Jesus commanded his followers to be baptized as an outward symbol of an inward commitment. That action puts the world on notice that we are leaving our old life behind and embracing the life God has for us. And it is a personal memorial of the day we fully committed ourselves to God.

That's why Jesus stood on the banks of the Jordan River that day. He was there to show us what baptism is all about. So where did Jesus go to be baptized? Perhaps a better question is, to whom did Jesus go? He went to John the Baptist—to a man consumed by God and leading others to be the same. Here we find our model of what baptism is and why it should be an element in the life of every person who desires to be a disciple of Jesus.

Then Jesus came from Galilee to the Jordan to be baptized by John. But John tried to deter him, saying, "I need to be baptized by you, and do you come to me?"

Jesus replied, "Let it be so now; it is proper for us to do this to fulfill all righteousness." Then John consented.

As soon as Jesus was baptized, he went up out of the water. At that moment heaven was opened, and he saw the Spirit of God descending like a dove and alighting on him. And a voice from heaven said, "This is my Son, whom I love; with him I am well pleased." (Matt. 3:13–17 NIV)

In this amazing scene, Jesus shows us what the heart of baptism is about. It's the mark of a life committed to God. In Jewish culture, people wash in a *mikvah*. In biblical times, this was a ritual bath in which you immersed yourself to be cleansed ceremonially so you could worship at the temple in Jerusalem. This was especially used as part of a ritual for those who were not Jewish and were converting to Judaism. They were baptized as a sign of dying to their old lives and entering into a new relationship with Yahweh, the God of Israel.

But there was a little problem—John was baptizing Jewish people. He was telling them to repent because the kingdom of God was at hand, and their Jewish heritage wasn't proof that they walked with God. So these committed people were baptized to signify their desire to really walk with God. That's why the religious people were angry. Baptizing Jews was outrageous—it was also unheard of! John was the only person doing this, which is how he got his nickname, *Yohanan the Baptizo*, John the Baptist, or more literally, John the Immerser.

Jesus's wanting to be immersed was a problem for John. Remember, John was telling people to repent, but Jesus had nothing to repent of. He's God. He doesn't have sins to confess or shameful deeds to wash away. This is why John was caught like a deer in the headlights.

I understand this feeling. I remember being asked to teach at a leadership conference, and my pastor introduced me and then sat down and started to take notes! I asked myself, "What's wrong with this picture?" I felt like a high school basketball coach teaching teenagers the fundamentals of the game, and Shaquille O'Neal shows up and wants to be part of the class. I'd say, "I think you should teach me!" (Unless it was the day we were learning to shoot free throws.)

But Jesus said, "I want to be baptized because it fulfills what God requires." Only then did John agree to baptize him. The issue for Jesus was to obey his Father and do what was right. Something happens when people decide to be baptized. They don't just decide to get wet; they are dying to the old way of life and craving to live the abundant life Jesus offers.

> Or have you forgotten that when we were joined with Christ Jesus in baptism, we joined with him in his death? For we died and were buried with Christ by baptism. And just as Christ was raised from the dead by the glorious power of the Father, now we also may live new lives. (Rom. 6:3–4)

May I See Some Identification?

Being baptized is not about getting dunked in a tank or performing some ritual. It's about deciding to be numbered with the disciples of Jesus. You see, people won't have a problem with someone going to church occasionally. But tell your non-Christian friends that you are being baptized, and they will think that you're taking this Jesus thing too far. Do you know why? Because they recognize how important baptism is, even though many in the church don't.

> Therefore, go and make disciples of all the nations, baptizing them in the name of the Father and the Son and the Holy Spirit. Teach these new disciples to obey all the commands I have given you. And be sure of this: I am with you always, even to the end of the age. (Matt. 28:19–20)

Jesus links baptism with following him. The issue isn't, "Can I still go to heaven if I'm not baptized?" The thief on the cross did, but he never had the chance to be baptized. I will go out on a limb and say that if they had taken him down from the cross and said, "Yes, that robbery was just a misunderstanding; please accept our deepest apologies and have a nice day," he would have been baptized.

If you are a disciple of Jesus, you will gladly obey him in this simple yet powerful act. I watch Christians go years without being baptized because they don't think it's a big deal. I say, "Jesus asks us to do this. That makes it a big deal!" Often, these people pray about God's will because they don't know what to do. We'll never figure out what God wants us to do if we haven't done what we know he's already asked us to do. Some say, "Well, I was baptized as an infant." So was I, but that kind of baptism is not what Jesus is talking about.

> The waters of baptism do that for you, not by washing away dirt from your skin but by presenting you through Jesus' resurrection before God with a clear conscience. (1 Pet. 3:21 Message)

I have pictures of my infant baptism, and I don't look like I had a clear conscience. In fact, it looked like I was screaming the entire time. I don't remember it, and it didn't signify anything in my life. So I cannot say I have obeyed Jesus in this area when that baptism was not of my volition.

Sometimes we hesitate because we're afraid. Something inside us knows what happens when we go in the waters of baptism. I can tell you from personal experience, people don't leave the same if they mean it. People repent before

God, declare their faith in Jesus, and commit to living out his purposes for their lives. I have had people hand me packs of cigarettes just before being baptized. They quit right on the spot—no patch, no gum, no hypnosis . . . nothing. It demonstrated their commitment to live for God starting from that moment.

One man who was getting baptized handed me his cigarettes while we were in the water. This baptism was at the ocean, and I thought that being a litterbug during a baptism wasn't the most spiritual thing to do. So I put the pack in my pocket and intended to throw it out when we got out of the water. Unfortunately, I forgot it was there. After I got home later that afternoon, Carey was washing the clothes I had been wearing at the baptism when she found the soaked pack of cigarettes in my pocket. She asked, "Bob, is there something about you that I don't know?" I told her the story.

Something happens when people who have prayed to receive Jesus decide to be watermarked by baptism. It shows their desire to live a revolutionary life by adding that element to their lives that Jesus and John had.

I was baptized when I had been a Christian for about four months, but in 1999 I traveled to Israel and visited the place where John baptized Jesus. I baptized twenty-five or thirty people in our tour group. At the end of the baptism service, I asked the other pastors to baptize me because I believed God was calling me to do something great. He was calling me to move to Miami and start a church. I was enjoying a good life. I worked at a big church and ran a college ministry full of students whose sole desire was to serve God. It was great. Yet I felt God stirring me and I couldn't shake it.

At that moment in the Jordan River, I did what Jesus did in that same spot. I decided to be consumed by God. I decided to live a life that wasn't comfortable but revolutionary. It's what God beckons all people to do who call Jesus Lord. He calls them to be watermarked and to start a revolution in their world by first starting one in their lives. At that moment, you will hear the words Jesus heard—the words of your loving heavenly Father who will look from heaven and say, "This is my son (or daughter), in whom I am well pleased."

6

Frequently Asked Questions

*H*opefully, the previous chapters have given you some fundamental truths about your decision to follow Christ and where to go from here. As a pastor, I'm often asked questions about Christianity and faith. Here are those most commonly asked.

What does it mean to be a Christian?

A Christian is a follower of Jesus. No one is born a Christian. Our sins separate us from God. Jesus reconciles us to God.

People decide to become Christians by asking Jesus to forgive them through his work on the cross. According to the Bible, once you've made that decision, you are a Christian. The goal then is to live for Jesus by following his example.

This is why reading the Bible is so important. You can't know how to live like Jesus if you don't know what Jesus did. As you open the Bible and learn about God, you will find God beginning to change you from the inside out. The Bible says, "God knew what he was doing from the very beginning. He decided from the outset to shape the lives of those who love him along the same lines as the life of his Son. The Son stands first in the line of humanity he restored. We see the original and intended shape of our lives there in him" (Rom. 8:29 Message).

Who is God?

A man named John, who was one of Jesus's disciples, said, "God is love" (1 John 4:8). The nature of God is love. The Bible also tells us that God is all-powerful (Isa. 40:25–26), all-knowing (Ps. 147:4–5), and ever-present (Jer. 23:23–24). God created everything (Gen. 1), and he desires a relationship with humankind, the pinnacle of his creation. That's why God asks us to call him Father.

This isn't the easiest question to answer, because God is greater than our language can even describe. That's why he came in the person of Jesus. Jesus said, "To see me is to see the Father" (John 14:9 Message), which leads us to our next question . . .

Who is Jesus?

We believe in one God who has revealed himself in three distinct persons: God the Father, God the Son, and God the Holy Spirit. Jesus is the Son of God, the second person of the Trinity.

Jesus is God in human flesh. He came to be the expression or explanation of who God is. The Bible says, "For the law was given through Moses, but God's unfailing love and faithfulness came through Jesus Christ. No one has ever seen God. But the unique One, who is himself God, is near to the Father's heart. He has revealed God to us" (John 1:17–18). Jesus came to die for our sins and create a way for you and me to have a relationship with God, but he also came to show us the character and nature of God.

> Christ is the visible image of the invisible God. He existed before anything was created and is supreme over all creation,

for through him God created everything in the heavenly realms and on earth. He made the things we can see and the things we can't see—such as thrones, kingdoms, rulers, and authorities in the unseen world. Everything was created through him and for him. He existed before anything else, and he holds all creation together. (Col. 1:15–17)

Who is the Holy Spirit?

Of all the members of the Trinity, the Holy Spirit is probably the least understood. God's Spirit is seen from the beginning of creation moving over the face of the waters (Gen. 1:2). The Holy Spirit works in our lives as Christians to draw us closer to God. Jesus said, "If you love me, obey my commandments. And I will ask the Father, and he will give you another Advocate, who will never leave you. He is the Holy Spirit, who leads into all truth" (John 14:15–17).

If you are a Christian, the Holy Spirit's presence is in your life. This is God's mark of ownership on every believer in Jesus. Paul the apostle wrote, "And when you believed in Christ, he identified you as his own by giving you the Holy Spirit, whom he promised long ago. The Spirit is God's guarantee that he will give us the inheritance he promised and that he has purchased us to be his own people. He did this so we would praise and glorify him" (Eph. 1:13–14).

The Holy Spirit constantly works in our lives. When the Holy Spirit is working in your life, changes begin to occur. Paul wrote, "But the Holy Spirit produces this kind of fruit in our lives: love, joy, peace, patience, kindness, goodness, faithfulness, gentleness, and self-control. There is no law against these things!" (Gal. 5:22–23).

Who is the devil?

When you think of the devil, don't think of a person wearing a red suit and holding a pitchfork. That's an inaccurate picture. The Bible gives us a different portrait of Satan. Satan was once an angel who served God, but he was filled with pride and banished from heaven (Isa. 14).

When he rebelled against God, he became known as Satan. The devil's name, Lucifer, means "bearer of light." Satan is not the equal of God. He's not even close to being as powerful as God is. Satan is a created being with limited power.

The good news is that the Bible says, "You, dear children, are from God and have overcome them, because the one who is in you is greater than the one who is in the world" (1 John 4:4 NIV). God's Spirit is greater than any of the devil's schemes. Satan will try to tempt us into not following

God's plan for our lives. He has been doing this from the beginning of creation (see Gen. 3). He is a deceiver who seeks to steal, kill, and destroy people's lives (see John 10).

The Bible is a big book. Where do I begin?

The best place to begin is in one of the Gospels. The Bible has four accounts of Jesus's life, and each looks at him from a different perspective. The shortest and easiest to read is the Gospel of Mark (the second Gospel). It was written to people who didn't have much Bible knowledge, so the writer explains in simple terms what happened in each situation. It is also only sixteen chapters, so by reading a chapter a day, you can be done in a little over two weeks.

Besides this, one habit I have is to read the book of Proverbs daily. Solomon, the son of King David, wrote the book of Proverbs. In this book, he shares the wisdom that each of us needs to make the right decisions as we face choices in our lives. Because the book of Proverbs has thirty-one chapters, and most months have thirty-one days, I read a chapter in Proverbs daily and ask God to give me wisdom as I go throughout my day.

After reading the Gospel of Mark, read Acts, the story of the early church. Then try to read the rest of the New

Testament. There might be things you don't understand. That's okay. Just focus on what you do understand and write down your questions. Take those questions to your small group or to your pastor. They can answer them for you.

What is an appropriate age for baptism?

Now as they went down the road, they came to some water. And the eunuch said, "See, here is water. What hinders me from being baptized?"

Then Philip said, "If you believe with all your heart, you may."

And he answered and said, "I believe that Jesus Christ is the Son of God."

So he commanded the chariot to stand still. And both Philip and the eunuch went down into the water, and he baptized him. Now when they came up out of the water, the Spirit of the Lord caught Philip away, so that the eunuch saw him no more; and he went on his way rejoicing. (Acts 8:36–39 NKJV)

Although the Bible does not address a specific age as a minimum requirement for baptism, the real issue is one of the heart. The passage quoted above gives us the requirement for baptism. It has nothing to do with age and everything to do with a person's spiritual condition. A person who understands that Jesus is the Son of God and who has decided to follow Jesus is a candidate for baptism. The age of the person depends on his or her ability to understand what is happening in baptism. This could be ten for one person and fourteen for another. A person seeking to be baptized must understand what baptism is and know why he or she is entering its waters. This cannot be an issue of religious duty or parental pressure, but must be a spiritual conviction resulting from a living faith in Jesus.

Am I a Christian if I don't get baptized?

Baptism is not a prerequisite for heaven, nor are we saved through baptism. The act of going into the water doesn't save us. Jesus saved us through his death on the cross and resurrection from the dead. When we place our faith in his finished work, it is then that we are saved.

> If you confess with your mouth that Jesus is Lord and believe in your heart that God raised him from the dead, you will be saved. For it is by believing in your heart that you are made right with God, and it is by confessing with your mouth that you are saved. (Rom. 10:9–10)

We are saved through faith, not works we do.

> For by grace you have been saved through faith, and that
> not of yourselves; it is the gift of God, not of works, lest
> anyone should boast. (Eph. 2:8–9 NKJV)

To believe that baptism saves us is to believe in a gospel that says our works make us right with God, which is not so according to Scripture. Baptism does not save you, but the saved are baptized. A person who has truly decided to follow Jesus will obey him. If one of his commands is to be baptized, then we should obey him, not because we believe it will save us but because we believe that our obedience pleases God.

Will I go to heaven if I am not baptized?

> Then one of the criminals who were hanged blasphemed
> Him, saying, "If You are the Christ, save Yourself and us."
> But the other, answering, rebuked him, saying, "Do
> you not even fear God, seeing you are under the same
> condemnation? And we indeed justly, for we receive the
> due reward of our deeds; but this Man has done nothing
> wrong." Then he said to Jesus, "Lord, remember me when
> You come into Your kingdom."

And Jesus said to him, "Assuredly, I say to you, today you will be with Me in Paradise." (Luke 23:39–43 NKJV)

The thief on the cross was not baptized and yet was given the promise of eternal life by Jesus. So baptism is not required for a person to go to heaven. However, I believe that if the thief on the cross had been given a chance to be baptized, he would have chosen to be obedient and follow Jesus's example.

Even though he was not baptized, it does not create an excuse for those of us who can obey God and seek baptism. A person who has only moments to live and calls out to God can be assured of salvation as this thief was, yet that should not inspire laziness or idleness for us in following the teachings of Jesus. Every person who can be baptized should be, not because heaven depends on it but because it expresses love for our Savior, who died for us. The least we can do is obey him in this simple yet powerful act.

What is communion?

Communion (also known as Eucharist or the Lord's Supper in some denominations) is an ordinance that began on the night before Jesus died on the cross. It is actually part of a Jewish feast called Passover. Passover is a celebration of God's deliverance of the Jewish people from slavery in Egypt. Every year all practicing Jews observe this most sacred ceremony.

In Jesus's day, this was no different. During the meal that commemorates the feast, Jesus picked up bread, broke it, and likened it to his body, which would be broken for us. Then he picked up a glass of wine and likened that to his blood, which would be shed for us.

The Bible records the scene this way:

> And he took bread, gave thanks and broke it, and gave it to them, saying, "This is my body given for you; do this in remembrance of me."
>
> In the same way, after the supper he took the cup, saying, "This cup is the new covenant in my blood, which is poured out for you." (Luke 22:19–20 NIV)

As Christians, we should regularly partake of communion to draw close to God and to celebrate our common faith. It is a reminder of the high price God paid for us to have a relationship with him—the life of his Son.

What translation of the Bible should I read?

There are many translations of the Bible for us to choose from. First, be assured they all say the same thing. It's not as though one translation says Jesus rose again and another translation says he didn't. Thankfully, they all say he did!

Translations vary for several reasons. Some translations—such as the King James Version, New King James Version, and New American Standard Bible—are written in a word-for-word format. The strength of these translations is that they provide highly accurate English translations of what was written in the Hebrew Old Testament and Greek New Testament.

Other translations—such as the New International Version, New Living Translation, and Contemporary English Version—seek to use "dynamic equivalence" in translating what is written in the original languages. They seek to not only translate the words but also provide the meaning of the words as they were used in their original form. For this reason, idioms and expressions are translated differently in dynamic equivalent translations than in word-for-word translations.

The result is the same, however; they seek to communicate God's heart as expressed through the pages of Scripture. The choice of which translation to read from comes down to personal preference. I own a copy of each of these translations and enjoy each. I read a word-for-word translation (NKJV) but encourage people to read others as well. Word-for-word translations are at a slightly higher reading level than dynamic equivalents, so your reading level might affect your choice.

All translations listed above are excellent translations and communicate the message of God as revealed through the Bible. Ultimately, it comes down to one thing: Which translation will you read regularly and comprehend the most?

How can I know what God wants me to do?

When we enter into a relationship with God, we inevitably ask, "What does God want me to do?" This can be as focused as a single decision or as broad as wanting to know what you should do with your life in general. Here's the good news: God has a plan for your life that is greater than anything you might imagine (see Eph. 3:20). The question is how to discover that plan and get in it!

There are several ways to discern what God wants. Here are the ones that have been most helpful to me over the years:

Examine what the Bible says. If the Bible speaks about this issue directly, then I can rest in knowing that

God would want me to obey what the Scriptures teach.

Seek guidance from your Christ-following friends. The Bible says, "Where there is no counsel, the people fall; but in the multitude of counselors there is safety" (Prov. 11:14 NKJV). When you are confronted with a decision and you aren't sure what to do, ask for input from people whom you respect, who love God and are passionately following Jesus. Generally, they will give you godly advice on how to deal with a situation.

Ask God for wisdom. The Bible says repeatedly that we should ask God for wisdom when we don't know what to do. The New Testament book of James says, "If you need wisdom, ask our generous God, and he will give it to you. He will not rebuke you for asking" (1:5). So whatever the problem, decision, or dilemma, if you ask God for wisdom, he'll give it to you. The great thing is that if the Bible says something about it, if your friends give you wise counsel, and if God gives you wisdom in the matter, you'll know what you should do.

Epilogue

Learning to Drive a Stick Shift

When I was sixteen, I got my first car—a 1982 Volkswagen Rabbit. It ran on diesel gas and broke down more times than I'd like to admit. I remember the day I got it. The car was gold, but years in the sun was turning it brown. It looked like C-3PO with a spray-on tan.

I paid the owner $400 for this rolling disaster, but you wouldn't have known from the smile on my face. My VW Rabbit brought me what every teenager desires most—freedom. All I had to do was learn how to drive it. My problem was I didn't realize the car had a stick shift when I purchased it.

I had never driven a car that wasn't an automatic transmission, so when I hopped into the car, I had a rude awakening. I put the key in the ignition, turned the car on, and the violent jerking that ensued made me think I was on an amusement park ride gone horribly bad. Noticing my plight, the former owner of my car got into the passenger seat and walked me through some simple steps to get my new car off his property.

He taught me what the clutch was and that this was crucial to shifting gears. He explained how to hear when the engine was ready for me to shift gears and accelerate. This driving lesson lasted fifteen minutes. Then he said, "You're ready to go." I told him that I still wasn't comfortable driving a stick and maybe he should give me a few more lessons. That's when he said, "Bob, the only way you learn to drive a stick shift is by getting behind the wheel and driving. There's no substitute for getting on the road, making mistakes, and learning as you go."

The same is true in our relationship with God. The only way to learn to walk with God is to walk with him. Will you make mistakes? Yes. You won't master the Christian faith in a day. It's a lifetime process of walking with Jesus as he molds us, shapes us, and changes us each day.

You'll be able to look back six months from now and see the progress you've made. I just passed my twenty-year mark as a follower of Jesus, and I can report to you that God has transformed my life far beyond anything I could have asked, thought, or imagined. He has been far kinder than I have deserved, and my goal each day—as it was on the day when I invited him into my life—is simply to walk with him.

That first year in my car, I stalled several hundred times and quickly burned out the clutch. But today, I'm good with a stick shift, and that thrust into the world of manual transmission forced me to get moving. My hope is that after reading this book, you start to walk and take steps of faith in God's direction. Your first place to start was here, but now it's time to go where God leads you by his grace. The joy is in the journey.

Notes

1. Frank Newport, "This Christmas, 78% of Americans Identify as Christian," Gallup, December 24, 2009, http://www.gallup.com/poll/124793/this-christmas-78-americans-identify-christian.aspx.

2. Dalia Sussman, "Poll: Elbow Room No Problem in Heaven," ABC News, December 20, 2005, http://abcnews.go.com/US/Beliefs/story?id=1422658.

3. William Barclay, *The Gospel of Matthew* (Louisville: Westminster John Knox, 1975), 225.

4. J. B. Philips, *The New Testament in Modern English* (New York: Touchstone Books, 1958), 140.

5. Rick Warren, *Rick Warren's Bible Study Methods* (Grand Rapids: Zondervan, 2006), 39.

Bob Franquiz is the founding and senior pastor of Calvary Fellowship in Miami, FL (www.calvarywired.com). Bob is also the founder of Church Ninja (www.churchninja .com), an organization that provides training and resources to pastors and church leaders. Bob's other books include *Elements: Starting a Revolution in Your World* and *Zero to Sixty: 60 Principles and Practices for Leading a Growing Church*. Prior to entering pastoral ministry, Bob played guitar for Christian hardcore band Strongarm, which has been called one of the best Christian metal bands of all time. Before planting Calvary Fellowship, Bob served as an assistant pastor at Calvary Chapel Fort Lauderdale, one of the ten largest churches in America. His primary role was dean of Calvary Chapel Bible College, where he trained future pastors, ministry leaders, and church planters. Bob considers his greatest achievement being married to Carey, his "just out of high school" sweetheart, for the last sixteen years. Together, they have three beautiful children: Mia, Alexander, and Olivia.

Made in United States
Orlando, FL
15 July 2022